ANIMALS
AROUND THE WORLD

DK

LONDON, NEW YORK, MUNICH,
MELBOURNE, AND DELHI

Written by Samantha Gray, Simon Holland,
Anna Lofthouse, Lorrie Mack, Caroline Stamps,
Fleur Star, Sarah Walker, Penelope York
Edited by Caroline Stamps
US editor Margaret Parrish
Designed by Mary Sandberg, Janet Allis,
Jacqueline Gooden, Tory Gordon-Harris,
Laura Roberts-Jensen, Clare Sheddon
Consultants Bryan and Cherry Alexander,
Kim Dennis-Bryan, Mark Fox, Nick Lindsay,
Derek Lyon, Paul Pearce-Kelly,
Sue Thornton, Barbara Taylor

Jacket designer Smiljka Surla
Picture researcher Rob Nunn
Production editor Sean Daly
Art director Rachael Foster
Publishing manager Bridget Giles

Content first published in various titles of the
Eye Wonder series in the United States between
2001 and 2007 by Dorling Kindersley.
This edition copyright © 2009 Dorling Kindersley

09 10 11 12 10 9 8 7 6 5 4 3 2 1

First published in the United States in 2009
by DK Publishing
375 Hudson Street, New York, New York 10014

A catalog record for this book
is available from the Library of Congress.

ISBN 978-0-7566-5818-2

Printed and bound by Hung Hing, China

Discover more at
www.dk.com

Contents

Introduction

There are an amazing variety of animals. Scientists split them into groups of animals that show similar features. The largest split is between vertebrates and invertebrates.

A bird is a vertebrate.

Vertebrates

These animals have a backbone.
They can be split up into five main groups.

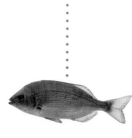

Mammals
Most mammals have fur. All mammals feed, or suckle, their young with milk produced by the mother.

Birds
have feathers and lay eggs. Most birds use their wings to flap and fly, but a few never fly.

Reptiles *have dry skin and scales. Most lay eggs, from which the young hatch.*

Amphibians
As adults, amphibians spend most of their lives on land. They return to water to breed.

Fish
have fins and scales and live in water. They breathe using their gills to take oxygen from the water.

Vertebrates

● Vertebrates make up about 5 percent of the animal kingdom.

● The largest group of vertebrates are the fish.

● Amphibians were the first vertebrates to live on land, some 370 million years ago.

Animals

A butterfly is an invertebrate.

Invertebrates

- Invertebrates make up about 95 percent of the animal kingdom.

- Most invertebrates are found in the oceans.

- Some invertebrates, such as corals, spend their adult lives in one place.

Invertebrates

These animals have no backbone. Invertebrates are broken down into more than 30 groups. The main groups are shown below.

Arachnids
have eight legs. They include spiders, scorpions, ticks, and mites.

Insects
have six legs. They include butterflies, moths, flies, beetles, and mosquitoes.

Crustaceans
have a hard outer shell. They include crabs, lobsters, and woodlice.

Mollusks
Most mollusks have a muscular foot. They include octopuses, squid, slugs, and snails.

Echinoderms
The word means "spiny skin." These animals include starfish and sea urchins.

Coral reefs are home to many animals, including vertebrates (such as fish) and invertebrates (such as the corals themselves).

Animal habitats

Animals live in all kinds of places or habitats, from icy Arctic wastes to hot, dry deserts. They show different adaptations to the particular habitat in which they live.

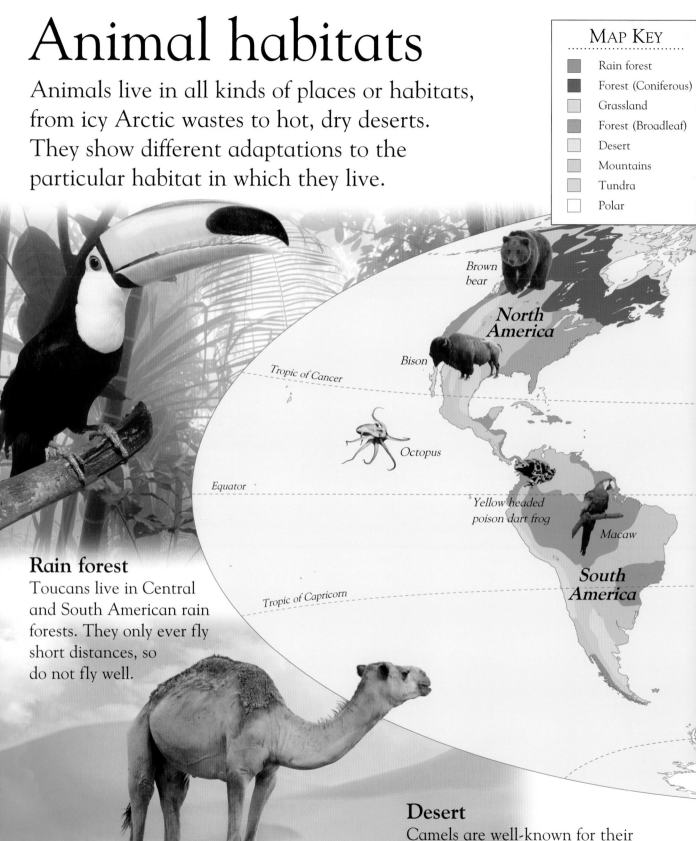

MAP KEY

▨	Rain forest
■	Forest (Coniferous)
▨	Grassland
▨	Forest (Broadleaf)
▨	Desert
▨	Mountains
▨	Tundra
☐	Polar

Brown bear

North America

Bison

Tropic of Cancer

Octopus

Equator

Yellow headed poison dart frog

Macaw

South America

Tropic of Capricorn

Rain forest
Toucans live in Central and South American rain forests. They only ever fly short distances, so do not fly well.

Desert
Camels are well-known for their ability to withstand the heat of a sandy desert, because they can survive long periods without water.

Oceans

Most of Earth is covered in water. The oceans are home to an incredible variety of animal life, including large sea turtles.

Polar regions

Polar bears live in the Arctic. Thick, cream-colored fur keeps them warm.

Polar bear

Arctic

Weasel

Europe

Wolf

Asia

China

Giant panda

Camel

Egyptian cobra

India

Africa

Tiger

Southeast Asia

Emperor angelfish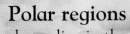

Gorilla

Zebra

Orangutan

African elephant

Shark

Kangaroo

Australia

Penguin

Antarctica

Grasslands

African grasslands (savannas) are home to herds of herbivores, which attracts large predators such as lions. A lion's sandy coat helps it blend into the grassland in which it hunts.

The ends of the Earth

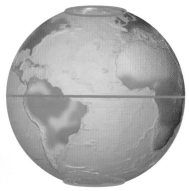

Earth is shaped like a big ball, or sphere. If you draw a line around its middle, the top half is the northern hemisphere and the bottom half is the southern hemisphere.

On top of the world...

The North Pole sits right at the top of the world. The icy area around it is known as the Arctic. Most of the Arctic is a huge sheet of frozen sea, with pieces of land around the edges.

CANADA

RUSSIAN FEDERATION

ARCTIC OCEAN

ARCTIC

North Pole

GREENLAND

LAPLAND

People

Lots of native peoples have adapted to life in the frozen Arctic. The Antarctic is too cold for humans, though, so only a few scientists call it home.

WINTER

In the middle of Arctic winter (end of December), none of the Sun's rays reach the North Pole, so there is never any daylight— it's always night.

Promised land

Antarctica is a very special place, where science has top priority and the environment is protected. No single country owns it, but lots of powerful ones meet to decide what happens there. This arrangement is called the Antarctic Treaty.

Arctic terns fly from the Arctic to the Antarctic and back again every year.

Antarctic oceans are covered with ice for most of the year.

SOUTHERN OCEAN

Weddell Sea

Antarctic Peninsula

ANTARCTICA

LESSER ANTARCTICA

South Pole

GREATER ANTARCTICA

Ross Ice Shelf

SOUTHERN OCEAN

...and down under

The South Pole is at the opposite end of the Earth, in Antarctica. Made of frozen land covered with ice and surrounded by (mostly) frozen sea, it has the driest, windiest, and coldest climate on Earth.

These penguins live in big groups called colonies.

Summer

At the same time, it's summer in the Antarctic, so the Sun never sets and daylight lasts for 24 hours. Arctic summer and Antarctic winter are at the end of June.

Animals

Like people, most animals find the Antarctic too cold to live in. But penguins like it there—they have a thick layer of feathers to keep them warm.

Life in the desert

Deserts are dry places where water and food are in short supply. Animals out searching for food during the day also have to cope with the extreme heat in hot deserts. So how do the animals survive?

The toad burrows backward, pushing sand away with its spadelike feet.

Food and drink

Many small antelopes, such as these springbok, graze on grasses and leaves. They get enough water to survive just from their food—but if given the chance they will also drink from pools.

Who needs to drink?

A spadefoot toad can stay under ground for months. It wraps itself in a cocoon of dried skin and lives off the water stored in its bladder.

When the feet on the ground get too hot, the lizard changes over.

Cool moves

Shovel snouted lizards keep cool by dancing! They lift up their feet two at a time to keep from burning them on the hot desert floor.

We've got it licked

Red kangaroos lick their forearms to beat the heat: when the saliva evaporates, it cools them down. They can also smell out water and will travel 125 miles (200 km) to find water during drought.

STOCKING UP

Camels survive in the desert through storing food—not by burying a stash, but by eating when they can and converting the food into fat, which the camel stores in its hump. Some other animals share this survival tip: both fat-tailed gerbils and Gila monsters (a species of lizard) store food in their tails.

Sidewinding snake species include some vipers and adders.

The snake curls up to make a loop, lifts the loop off the sand, and throws it forward to move along.

Making tracks

Sidewinder snakes don't slither forward, but travel sideways in an S-shape. This way, only part of the snake's belly comes into contact with the hot sand.

The tracks show where the snake lifts up and sets down.

Taking a dive

Sand skinks are also called sandfish because they "swim" through the sand. The sand is a little cooler just beneath the surface, and it's also a safe place to hide.

Forest facts

● Tropical rain forests only cover a small area of the world (7%).

● Over half the world's wildlife lives in the rain forests.

● The largest area of tropical rain forest is the Amazon jungle in South America.

● Jungle soil is shallow, only 4 in (10 cm) deep, yet some of the tallest trees in the world grow in it.

FRAGILE FORESTS

Rain forests help to clean the world's air and water. Jungle plants give us medicines that make us well when we are ill. Rain forests are very important  but are shrinking every day – chopped down for land and wood. We need to value these amazing forests, and take care of all the animals that live in them.

Welcome to the jungle

Monkeys call loudly from giant trees, huge spiders scuttle across your feet, and insects as big as dinner plates buzz around your ears. You're in the jungle!

Where in the world...

Tropical rain forests are found on either side of the equator – an imaginary line that circles the globe like a belt. The weather near the equator provides perfect conditions for lush forests to grow.

Weather forecast

It's easy to guess the daily weather forecast in the jungle – hot and humid with heavy rain. Some areas of tropical rain forests get a massive 160 in (4 m) of rain each year and the temperature is always between 75 and 80 °F (24-27 °C).

Shades of green

Getting lost in the rain forest can be a real problem. The best way to travel through it is by boat. Many rivers snake through the jungle, carrying excess rainwater toward the sea.

Animal magic

There is an incredible amount of different animals living in tropical rain forests. They are mostly very shy, however, and are experts at doing disappearing acts among the leaves.

Baby gorillas, like this one, live with their families in African jungles.

The blue planet

Oceans cover more than two thirds of the Earth's surface. In this vast underwater world, many sea creatures live together, often hidden beneath the waves.

The Pacific Ocean covers more than one third of the Earth's surface.

Gulls swoop down from the sky to scoop up a fishy snack.

Fishing for food

Oceans are a source of food for seabirds, who fly or swim in search of fish.

Sea turtles

There are many types of sea creatures, including reptiles such as turtles. These have to rise to the surface to breathe. They breathe air through their nostrils.

Green turtles live in warm waters in the Atlantic, Indian, and Pacific Oceans.

One big ocean

If you traveled in a boat, you could sail to every ocean and sea because they all join up. It could be said that there is really only one vast ocean.

Fishy facts

- The largest areas of seawater are called oceans. The smaller ones are called seas.

- Wind creates waves on the ocean surface. Strong winds make bigger waves.

- All seawater is salty. One of the saltiest seas is the Red Sea.

Plankton

The sunlit ocean teems with tiny life forms called plankton. These are a vital food source for many sea creatures.

From space, Earth looks blue because water covers so much of its surface.

Breathing through blowholes

Whales are mammals. Unlike fish, they cannot breathe underwater. They surface to breathe air through their blowholes. Blue whales are the largest mammals of all.

Life in a coral reef

Coral reefs teem in the daytime
with beautiful and bizarre
creatures. At night, many retreat
into caves to rest. Now a new
party begins! Different fish leave
their hideouts to look for food.

Underwater angels
With their slim bodies, emperor
angelfish can dart in and out
of gaps in the coral. Angelfish
partners stay together for life.

SEA SERPENT STORIES

Tales of man-eating sea serpents once
made people wary of eels. Today,
divers still tell stories of moray eels
gripping them in their toothy jaws.
Divers mostly have only
themselves to blame. Some poke
their hands into coral-reef caves.
This can give an eel resting at
home an unwelcome surprise!

Lettuce leaf

Like other sea slugs, lettuce slugs are related to garden snails. These frilly slugs may look like salad, but their skin produces a slime that tastes revolting.

Coral reefs offer many hiding places for small fish escaping from larger predators.

A twist of the tail

To anchor themselves, sea horses twist their tails around coral. If an enemy appears, they change color to match their surrounding.

Sea horses are among the tiniest fish in a coral reef.

Slippery as an eel

Moray eels have slimy, snakelike bodies. They slither into caves and crevices to hide during the day. Their pointed faces peer out from the coral. At night, they hunt for food.

House-hunting hermits

Hermit crabs often make their homes inside the empty shells of other animals. They may also move into small caves in the coral reef.

Mammal world

You might wonder if tiny mice, huge whales, and humans have anything in common. They do – they are all mammals! All mammals have hair or fur, are warm-blooded and have a constant body temperature, and feed their young on milk.

Odd eggs out

Most mammals are born, but the hedgehoglike echidnas (see right) and the duck-billed platypus hatch from eggs.

Instant food

Almost all female mammals suckle their young on milk. The milk provides the best balance of fat and protein so that young mammals can grow quickly.

Hair (or fur) helps to keep heat in.

The human species is just one of the 4,000 or so

Kid mammals

Humans belong to a group of mammals called primates. Other primates include monkeys and apes, so they are our closest mammal relatives.

Open wide

Hippopotamuses would be perfect at the dentist's with a large mouth and a wide jaw stretch. All mammals have distinct jaws, meaning that the lower jaw is hinged directly to the skull.

incredible mammal species on the planet Earth.

Mammals are the only animals to have ear flaps.

19

Family life

Some mammals choose to stay in family groups, making it easier for them to find food and defend themselves. Mammal parents spend longer with their young than other animals.

Playtime tussles
Female lions live in permanent groups called prides and look after each other's cubs. The cubs play-fight, which is how they learn to hunt.

Meerkat watch

A gang of meerkats varies from five to 30 members. They are very protective of their home, or territory, and have different roles, such as sentry duty or babysitting.

African elephants are the biggest land mammals.

Amazing mammals

- There are about 60,000 muscles in an elephant's trunk.

- A lion can devour 50 lb (23 kg) of meat in one meal. That's about 350 hotdogs.

- Ferocious fights can happen between rival meerkat gangs.

An elephant's tusks are just overgrown teeth.

Female families

Female elephants and their children stay close together in family herds. The biggest female, the matriarch, leads them wherever they go.

Different diets

What do you prefer? Vegetables, meat, fish, or a little of everything? Mammals eat all kinds of things. They eat because they need energy, just like a car needs fuel to go.

A mixed plate

This Alaskan brown bear, like other brown bears, eats a meat and plant, or omnivorous, diet. It waits to pounce on any salmon swimming upstream, but also chomps on plants, fungi, and large insects.

Wild mammals build their daily routine around finding enough to eat.

Keep on chewing

American bison are herbivores, which means they only eat plants. They graze on grass. Then they rest. Then they chew on the grass even more.

Make mine meat

A pack of gray wolves maul their hunting prize. As one of the world's best-known carnivores, or meat eaters, their bodies are designed for hunting other animals. They have powerful jaws and sharp teeth.

Don't stick your tongue out!

Giant anteaters wouldn't listen to this warning. They use their 2 ft (60 cm) spiked and sticky tongues to ensnare termites and ants once their clawed front feet have ripped open the nests.

The anteater pushes its long, tubelike snout into the hole.

Amazing mammals

● Wolves can eat up to 20 lb (9 kg) of meat in one meal.

● A giant anteater flicks out its tongue 150 times a minute.

● Brown bears eat a lot. The extra weight helps them survive the winter, when they sleep, or hibernate, for several months.

Amazing marsupials

Kangaroos and koalas belong to a group of mammals called marsupials. A marsupial is only partly formed when it is born, and it continues to grow in a pocket, called a pouch, on the outside of its mother's stomach.

Mobile homes

A baby kangaroo or joey is born after just 12 days inside its mother. It crawls through its mother's fur and into a special place called a pouch. It stays in its mother's pouch, drinking her milk, for the next six months.

When the kangaroo hops, a long tail helps it to balance.

Thirsty work

A newborn kangaroo is blind, helpless, and very pink. It clings tightly to its mother's fur and will suckle continually.

Piggyback, please

A koala spends most of its life in eucalyptus trees. It sleeps for up to 18 hours a day and feeds only on eucalyptus leaves. A baby koala lives in its mother's pouch for about six months before crawling onto her back.

A fully grown kangaroo is as tall as an adult human, but at birth, it is less than ¾ inch (2 cm) long.

Powerful kangaroos

The largest living marsupials, red kangaroos live in Australia. They live in groups of about two to 10 animals, with one dominant male and several females. When bounding at full speed, kangaroos can reach speeds of about 30 mph (50 kph).

WINNER TAKES THE GIRL

Male kangaroos sometimes fight over females. This fighting can take the form of "boxing." The kangaroos stand up on their hind legs and attempt to push their opponent off balance by jabbing him or locking forearms. The winner of the boxing match is the stronger male, and he gets the girl!

The high life

Bats are the only flying mammals, and there are about 1,000 species in the bat family. These furry fliers are divided into two groups: the small, mainly meat-eating microbats, and the large, mainly vegetarian megabats.

Night fliers

A colony of Mexican fruit bats awakes at dusk and flies off to feed on fruit and nuts. All bats are nocturnal mammals.

The biggest bat

The flying fox is the largest bat in the world, with a wing span of over 5 ft (1.5 m). It feeds on fruit and pollen.

oosting together

ts often gather together in huge numbers at a
gle site. This may be a cave, an old building, or
ollow tree. The site must provide the bats with
lter and protection from predators.

FINDING FOOD

Most insect-eating bats hunt using a process called
echolocation. Each bat makes a series of clicks, and
this sound is carried out into the air. This noise
bounces off any potential prey, such as mosquitoes
and moths, and sends information back to the bat.
The bat can then find the prey, and enjoy its meal!

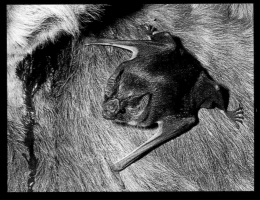

Bloodsucker

This vampire bat is enjoying a
tasty snack of donkey blood. Its
sharp teeth easily pierce the skin,
and its spit prevents the blood
from clotting. Only three species
of bat feed on blood.

Tent making bats

These tiny fur balls are Honduran
white bats. They only appear
white under artificial light and
are well camouflaged in the murky
rain forest. They create shelters
from large rain-forest leaves.

I spy a bird's nest

Stoats are fierce hunters, pouncing on small rodents and mammals they find. They will also grab an opportunity to steal and eat birds' eggs.

A particular diet

This black-footed ferret has a limited diet, which is rare among carnivores. It largely hunts prairie dogs, small North American rodents.

Cunning carnivores

If asked to name a carnivore (or meat eater), you would probably think of a big cat such as a lion or a tiger. But there are plenty of smaller meat eaters.

Sharp teeth are designed for tearing into flesh.

Meat?
Skunks hunt small mammals, lizards, snakes, and insects. But they also eat plants, fungi, and berries, which makes them omnivores ("everything eaters").

A meat-eating marsupial
The Tasmanian devil has jaws powerful enough to crush bone. It hunts by night, using a strong sense of smell to root out snakes, lizards, and whatever else it can find.

Meat!
Hyenas eat a diet that is largely made up of meat, so they are carnivores. They have incredibly powerful jaws, for tearing through fur and crushing bone.

Hyenas often feast on carrion.

These small jackals are trying to grab a bit of the meat.

Cat comparisons

The whole feline family shares certain physical features and characteristics. A pet cat creeping up on its prey in the yard behaves in a very similar way to a big cat stalking and hunting its prey in the wild.

Treetop rest
Cats have the ability to perch in the most difficult places. A long tail helps the animals to balance, and paws are spread out to support weight. All young cats have to learn to climb, and usually have a few accidents along the way!

Fit as a feline

Cats don't need to exercise to stay in shape. When they stretch and roll, their muscles receive a thorough workout.

Cat facts

● A cat's tail clearly shows what mood it is in. It will be lashed around when angry, or raised high when greeting or exploring new places.

● Cats swallow their food without chewing, as they don't have any grinding teeth.

On the prowl

All cats have a strong hunting instinct, and wild cats must kill in order to survive. Well-fed domestic cats have food provided, but the urge to hunt is not easily forgotten.

Cat calls

The leopard is one of the four roaring cats, along with the tiger, lion, and jaguar. The other big cats can growl and make chirping noises. Cats' noises communicate their feelings, and meowing, purring, growling, or roaring indicate a wide range of emotions.

Supersenses

Most cats hunt alone and at night so they constantly rely on their highly tuned supersenses. Sight, smell, hearing, taste, and touch are all much more highly developed in cats than in humans.

Sound
Large, funnel-shaped ears draw sound into them. Cats can hear even the smallest of noises, which helps them to detect potential prey.

Sight
Cats have excellent eyesight and can see up to six times better than humans in dim light.

A special sense
Cats have a special organ in the roof of their mouths, called the Jacobson's organ. This allows them to "taste" smells. When the cat curls back its lips (a process known as "flehming"), it can analyze scents that other cats have left behind.

Bright eyes

Cats are known for their brilliant eyesight, and eyes that glow in the darkness. When it is dark, cats' pupils expand to let in lots of light so the cats can see. The pupils then narrow again when it is brighter.

Narrow pupils in the light.

Expanded pupils in the dark.

Touch

Whiskers are long, stiff hairs with nerve endings at the roots. Framing the cat's face, these hairs help it to feel its way around, by providing the cat with information about its environment.

Smell

A sensitive nose helps each cat to recognize its home, mate, family, and food. A cat's nose has about 19 million nerve endings in it.

Taste

A large, rough tongue is used for grooming, licking meat from bones, and lapping up water.

SENSITIVE SENSES

All cats are extremely sensitive to vibrations in the air. Some may even sense earthquake tremors and volcano eruptions before they occur. People living on the slopes of Mount Etna, an active volcano in Italy, often keep pet cats as early warning devices. When the cats run away in terror, their owners quickly follow!

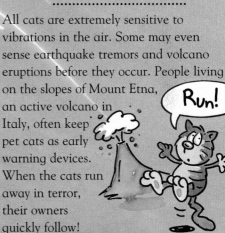

Run!

Speed king

The cheetah is unusual compared to the other big cats, which have large, sturdy bodies. Built for speed and agility, the cheetah has a small head, a long, streamlined body, and thin, powerful legs. Swift and slender, it is the fastest land animal in the world.

A crying cat

The distinctive black stripes on a cheetah's face are often referred to as tear stripes. It is possible that these help to reduce the glare of the sun.

Can't catch me!

The cheetah can reach its maximum speed of about 70 mph (112 kph) in under three seconds. This is faster than a sports car can accelerate. Not surprisingly, it can only keep up this pace for a few minutes.

CHEETAH TRAINING

Although it seems odd now, in the 16th century cheetahs were often caught when young and trained to help huntsmen kill antelope and gazelle. Cheetahs were sent after prey and, after knocking the animal down, would wait for their owners to complete the kill and remove the body.

Watchful cheetah

Cheetahs tend to have large territories. They need to keep a constant watch over their area, as competition for food and space is fierce.

Due to its build and speed, the cheetah is often compared to the greyhound.

Motherly love

To prevent the cubs from being killed by predators when they are young, the mother moves them to new locations on a daily basis. The cubs are covered in spiked fur when they are small. This camouflages them in the grass, and makes them look bigger.

Leader of the pack

From a tiny chihuahua to the mighty wolf, members of the dog family vary enormously in size. In the wild most are pack animals, for company, for power when hunting, and for protection.

A wolf's long snout contains 42 teeth, including four pointed canines.

Wolves are the ancestors of the domestic dog.

Who's out there?
A coyote will howl to communicate. A long howl lets other animals know where you are. It also tells other packs to avoid an area, to limit any confrontation.

Staying together
One male and one female rule a wolf pack, while other pack members know their place in a strict pecking order.

I'll look after you!

Cubs need a lot of care in their first year. Ethiopian wolf females such as this one tend to take turns suckling and caring for the young in their pack.

Fox cubs spend a lot of their time playing with each other.

I win! I win!

Like other cubs, young foxes learn a lot of their hunting skills by play fighting.

Wolves are accomplished hunters, with excellent senses.

A wolf's thick coat protects it from freezing conditions.

Bear necessities

With their strong bodies, thick legs, five-clawed feet, and dense fur, there is no mistaking a bear. Aside from the polar bear, most bears live in forests.

A bear will always climb downward bottom first.

It's cozy in here
Polar bears survive the freezing Arctic with hollow, heat-trapping hairs, and a layer of fat under the skin. Cubs are born in snow dens, and spend their first months well insulated from the icy conditions.

Remember to look up!
Bears are surprisingly agile climbers and haul themselves up trees to find honeycombs or fruit. Cubs may climb to avoid predators.

Bears have poor eyesight and poor hearing.

Bear facts

- Bears will try to intimidate rivals by standing up and walking on their back legs.

- A bear will not eat or create waste while it is in hibernation.

- Bears only have short tails.

Fishing bear

Brown bears will line up at particular rivers at certain times of the year waiting for salmon to leap up river. They catch these large fish in their mouths.

Bamboo bear

Pandas have a limited diet and only eat bamboo. Bamboo is not very nutritious, so pandas have to spend a lot of time eating to get enough energy to keep them going.

Insect bear

A Sun bear uses its strong curved claws to rip open ants' nests and beehives. Then it will slurp up the contents with its extremely long tongue.

Rodent success

Rodents are a hugely successful group of mammals, as shown by the fact that they live on all continents except for Antarctica. Most rodents live in social groups.

A typical rodent

Brown rats have many features associated with rodents. They have long whiskers, long snouts, beady eyes, and large ears. Their senses of sight and hearing are excellent. They also have long front teeth.

All rodents have four long incisors. A beaver's are orange.

Gnaw it up

All rodents use their powerful jaws for gnawing. Perhaps the most spectacular example of this is the beaver. Beavers build huge dams and lodges from trees they have felled with their teeth.

Rodent giants

The capybara is the world's largest rodent. Huge groups will live near swamps, lakes, and rivers. (It may look unlikely, but this rodent can swim! It even has partially webbed toes.)

A prickly rodent

This rodent has an effective defense against possible predators. If threatened, a Cape porcupine will raise its spines and rush backward at the predator. Those spines are sharp, and they work as a deterrent!

A porcupine's spines, or quills, can be up to 14 in (35 cm) in length.

Smaller rodents are good climbers.

A sleepy rodent

"Dor" means "sleeping." The hazel dormouse hibernates for some seven months each year, in a cozy nest that insulates it from the cold. It keeps a handy store of food in case it needs a bite to eat.

A tree-loving rodent

Squirrels are known for their climbing skills. The red squirrel shown here is one of the few rodents to live alone (except when a female has her young).

Primate party

Apes, monkeys, and humans are the most well-known members of a mammal group called primates. A primate party would be a swinging one since primates are playful and highly intelligent creatures.

A devoted mother

An orangutan mother and baby stay together for about eight years. The baby clings to its mother's fur as she moves through the trees. At night the mother makes nests from leaves for her baby and her to sleep in.

Gentle giants

Gorillas live in family groups. They weigh in as the heaviest of all the primates, but despite appearances are peaceful vegetarians. Their enthusiasm for eating forest plants can result in large pot bellies.

A gripping tail

Many Central and South American monkeys – such as this black howler monkey – use their grasping, or prehensile, tail as a fifth limb. With its very distinctive howl, it is one of the loudest primates.

Second in the class

Humans score highest for intelligence but chimpanzees are second. This chimp is using a stone as a tool for cracking open palm nuts.

Amazing mammals

● The orangutan's name comes from the Malay words for "man of the wood."

● Do you like making faces? Many primates can make faces to show their feelings and to communicate with each other.

If you scratch my back...

...I'll scratch yours. These baboons are checking each other's fur for ticks and lice. It is part of a behavior shared by most primates called grooming. This also helps the primates to develop good friendships.

Life on the hoof

Hoofed animals are herbivores, and spend lots of time grazing. In the wild most are hunted by large predators, so they are built to run.

Rhinocerous
Not all hoofed animals are under threat from predators: the rhino is just too big to tackle.

Quick escape
Goats are surprisingly agile, and can even climb trees to escape a predator. People keep goats to supply meat, wool, milk, cheese, and leather.

Different giraffes have different markings.

Lofty heights
Giraffes are the world's tallest land animals, reaching 18 ft (5.5 m). They graze leaves from trees.

Horned attack
Gemsbok have horns that can reach 5 ft (1.5 m) in length. They are rarely used as the threat of use is usually enough.

Gemsbok live in desert regions.

Safety in numbers

Many hoofed animals live in herds. It means there are more pairs of eyes looking out for danger, and less chance of one animal losing its life to a predator. Zebra herds can contain hundreds of individuals.

Zebra and wildebeest mingle in the Serengeti National Park, Tanzania.

Marine mammals

Asked to name a marine mammal, most people will probably say a whale. Sea otters and polar bears are mammals that spend an awful lot of their time in the water—but, unlike whales and dolphins, they can also walk around on land.

Sailors have long called sea otters the "old men of the sea" because of their white whiskers and expressive faces.

What's for dinner?
Sea otters hunt in kelp forests for a range of seafood. They love to eat sea urchins, but will also munch on crabs, fish, squid, and mussels.

Sea otters spend most of their time in the sea.

Fur, fur, and more fur
Sea otters have incredibly dense fur, which keeps them warm. In a patch of fur the size of your fingernail, there are about 100,000 hairs—that's the same as the number of hairs on a human head!

Polar bears have been known to swim about 60 miles (100 km) in one stretch.

A polar bear lashes out as an Arctic fox, which is a land mammal, scoots by.

At home in the snow

A polar bear has hollow hairs, which keep the heat in. Combined with a thick layer of bear fat, they do not feel the cold of their Arctic home. If anything, they overheat!

Bear in the water

Polar bears are excellent swimmers, using their webbed paws to pull them along. In fact, their Latin name means "sea bear."

The otters anchor themselves to sea kelp.

Sea otters spend much of their time lying on their backs. They will even sleep and eat like this!

Fun in the water

These marine mammals are seals.
Although they come onto land
to rest and to give birth, they
are most at home in the water,
where they perform graceful
underwater acrobatics.

True seals swim by moving their back flippers from side to side.

The short front flippers are used to steer the seal.

Eared seals have much longer front flippers than true seals.

Which are you?

Seals can be divided into two
groups: true (or earless) seals
and eared seals. True seals,
such as these harbor seals,
have no external ears.

What about eared seals?

Eared seals, such as this sea lion,
have small external ears. They
can also move around more easily
on land and support themselves
in a semi-upright position.

Breaking away

Harp seal pups triple their weight in the 12 days after their birth. Their mother then abandons them. After a month, they begin to lose their white coat for the adult gray fur.

Seals have often been mistaken for swimmers. Many legends tell of them coming ashore and behaving like people.

Like many mammals, seals like to play. It's a good way to learn.

Which is the biggest of all?

Male elephant seals are the largest of all seals, growing to 20 ft (6 m) and weighing more than 3½ tons (3 tonnes).

The male elephant seals are some 10 times heavier than the females.

Gentle sea cows

In warm, shallow waters, large sea mammals called dugongs and manatees live a peaceful life. They have no natural enemies, eat only plants, and never fight.

Dugongs and manatees lived in the oceans during the age of the dinosaurs.

Dugongs often dig down into the sand to eat sea grass roots.

Funny face
Like manatees, this dugong has no front teeth! Its teeth grow only along the sides of its mouth. Flippers steer and scoop up food.

Underwater lawnmower
Dugongs and manatees are the only vegetarian sea mammals. They swim slowly, grazing on sea grass.

Manatees sometimes have algae growing on their backs.

Noises in the night
Dugongs relax during the day and spend most of the night eating. Like manatees, they are noisy eaters. There are loud sounds of chomping teeth and flapping lips!

Sea grass beds are good feeding grounds.

Motherly love

Dugongs and manatees give birth to only one calf every three to five years. The newborn calf rises to the surface immediately for its first breath of air. It stays with its mother for up to two years, clinging to her or resting on her back.

Calf stays close to its mother.

Fishy facts

- Dugongs have a tail that is pointed at the ends. Manatees have a paddle-shaped tail.

- On meeting, sea cows grab each other's flippers then put their mouths together to kiss.

- Manatees and dugongs can live for as long as 60 years.

Leap in the deep

The ocean-dwelling cetaceans are some of the most specialized mammals in the world. The cetacean family includes all whales, dolphins, and porpoises. All have streamlined bodies, can dive deeply, and can hold their breath underwater for long periods of time.

Leaping high
Bottlenose dolphins are found in all of the world's oceans, except the polar regions. Living in groups, or schools, of between four and 20 animals, these playful mammals often leap above the waves.

Amazing mammals

- There are two types of whales. Baleen whales, which filter food through plates in their mouths, and toothed whales, such as killer whales.

- All cetaceans breathe through nostrils on their heads.

- Water supports a whale's weight; if whales lived on land they would be too big to survive.

- A humpback whale calf can grow until it is approximately 50 ft (16 m) long.

Breaching giants

This humpback whale is leaping high out of the water. This leaping is known as breaching. All whales breach, and we don't really know why they do this. It may be to warn off other whales, to communicate with their group, or just for fun. A whale this enormous will make a huge splash when it hits the water.

Water baby

Humpback whales tend to have their calves in the spring, in warm, tropical waters. The calf is born tail first, and its mother helps it to the surface so it can breathe. The calf will stay with its mother for about a year.

All about birds

There are about 9,000 different species of birds living on Earth, and all evolved from reptiles millions of years ago. Birds live in almost every part of the world, from the icy Antarctic to steamy tropical rain forests.

Birds have wings instead of arms.

Birds have a strong horny beak and no teeth.

Lightweight skeleton

This is a crow's skeleton. As with all flying birds, its bones are hollow, like straws. Solid bones would make birds too heavy to fly.

This bird bone has a honeycomb structure.

Ulna, a wing bone.

Wishbone

Scaly toes and feet.

On the inside

Birds cannot chew food as they do not have any teeth. Instead they have a special grinding organ called a gizzard, which is a part of the stomach. Food is crushed as it passes through the gizzard.

The keel anchors the wing muscles.

The ankle bone.

Fancy flier

As with all birds of prey, this red-tailed hawk is a powerful flyer. The wings are large and strong, allowing the hawk to fly and soar for many hours at a time. Wing shape and size varies hugely between bird species.

Down feather

Body feather

Flight feather

Useful feathers

Feathers are essential for flight, but they also keep birds warm, act as camouflage, and can be used in mating displays. Each bird has several different types of feathers, including down, body, and flight feathers.

Almost too small to see!

The tiny bee hummingbird weighs only 0.05 oz (1.6 g) and is smaller than some insects in its rain forest home. The largest bird in the world is the ostrich.

Feathery facts

- There are many millions of birds living on Earth.

- Only birds, bats, and insects are capable of powered flight.

- All birds have feathers, even those that cannot fly.

The plumed whistling-duck is a waterfowl.

The stunning scarlet ibis is a wading bird.

The chaffinch is a perching song bird.

Different birds

The many thousands of bird species are divided into specific families. The families include birds of prey, songbirds, parrots, waterfowl, and waders.

Eggs and hatching

A female bird lays eggs, then she or the male bird sits on them to keep them warm. When a chick is ready to hatch, it faces the egg's round end and begins to peck its way through the shell.

Breaking out

A duckling has a special egg tooth, which it uses to break through the eggshell. The tooth falls off once the duckling has hatched.

Protective parent

Like some other birds, emperor geese lay their eggs in nests on the ground. They spend 24 days keeping the eggs warm before their chicks hatch. Parents also have to be on guard to protect their eggs from hungry predators.

Wood thrushes eat fruit, insects, and juicy-looking grubs like these.

Free at last

This tired duckling has spent over a day chipping its way through the shell. Now that it has tumbled out, its feathers are still wet. Soon they will dry out and become fluffy.

Begging beaks

These wood thrush chicks beg for food with their beaks wide open. Until they can fly, they rely on their parents to bring them food. They eat a lot and grow quickly.

Caring for chicks

Parent birds feed their chicks and guard them from harm until they can fend for themselves. Ducklings and some other newly hatched chicks can run, swim, and even find food. Most chicks hatch naked, blind, and helpless.

Free-falling fledglings

Mandarin ducks nest in a hole in a tree, high in the air. When all the eggs are hatched, the mother calls to the chicks from the ground. Each chick crawls out of the hole, launching itself freefall. Amazingly all the chicks land unhurt. They follow their mother to find food. Mandarin ducks wade and feed in woodland ponds and rocky streams.

Each newly hatched duckling jumps from the tree.

Swanning around

Young swans are called cygnets. With their short necks and fluffy gray feathers, they do not yet look like their beautiful parents. Cygnets can swim, but they may ride on their mother's back!

Keeping cozy

In winter, the female emperor penguin lays a single egg then leaves for the sea. The male holds the egg off the ice on his feet. After the chick hatches, the male keeps it warm until the female returns.

Foster parent

This young cuckoo is larger than the wren feeding it. Cuckoos lay their eggs in other birds' nests. When it hatches, the cuckoo flings out the other eggs. Now it will get all the food.

Colorful chorus
The unusual song of male gouldian finches is made up of hisses, clicks, and long, shrill sounds. Living together in flocks, rainbow-colored gouldian finches are sociable birds.

Star performer
The nightingale sings loudly and musically. Its low, long notes are particularly haunting. Singing fearlessly through the day and night, the nightingale is not a shy bird.

Songbirds
Some birds sing particularly musical and enchanting songs. They are called songbirds, and the best known is the nightingale. Songbirds have a special voice box, called a syrinx, with thin walls that vibrate as they sing. In this way, they produce more complex and beautiful sounds than other birds.

The nightingale's special voice box allows it to sing its haunting song.

Street singer
The warbling song of European robins proclaims their territory. After pairs form to breed, only the male sings. Under streetlights, he may sing into the night.

Feathery facts

● During the breeding season, male songbirds use their song to entice females and warn away other males.

● The mockingbird can imitate snatches of songs from 20 or more other bird species, all within a few minutes!

Singing a love song

At dusk, the song thrush finds a treetop perch and delivers its powerful song. Males looking for a mate give the longest performances. They may also deliver a battle song when competing with other males.

Amazing owls

Most owls wake up as dusk falls. They preen themselves, combing their heads with their claws. Velvety flight feathers muffle the flapping of their wings as they take to the skies. Their hoots, screeches, and whistles break the silence of the night.

Invisible owl

In woodland, owls slumber in trees during the day. Their brownish feathers blend in with the bark. This great horned owl has tufts of feathers that look like horns.

Spectacular!

Spectacled owls have markings that look like a pair of spectacles around their eyes. The young have the opposite coloring of the parents and are white with black spectacles.

As white as snow
Sometimes called Arctic owls or ghost owls, snowy owls change color with the seasons from gray-brown to white. In the snow, a white owl can sneak up on prey unseen.

Turning heads
Owls have forward-looking eyes. To see to the side or back, this barn owl must turn its head. It can swivel its head a long way around.

Swift and silent
Sweeping silently through the skies, eagle owls listen intently for small sounds. Their prey may not even hear them approach as they swoop down to sink in their talons.

Wonderful waterfowl

Lakes, ponds, rivers, and other freshwater areas are a favorite place for waterfowl such as ducks, geese, and swans to live. There are many different species of these water-loving birds, which can be found around the world.

Life by the sea

The emperor goose lives in ponds and marshes close to the sea. These geese are very noisy, communicating frequently with the rest of the flock. Emperor geese eat some shellfish, as well as grasses.

Sociable swans

Mute swans are sociable creatures, and many may live in a small area. To begin flying, these large birds use the water as a runway, flapping their wings and running along the surface of the water until they finally take off.

Distinguished ducks

These black-bellied whistling ducks make a very shrill whistling sound! These vocal birds live in small flocks and are easily recognisable with their bright pink beaks.

Feathery facts

- Most birds have between 1,500 and 3,000 feathers, but some swans can have over 25,000 feathers.

- All waterfowl have webbed feet. These act as flippers, pushing the birds through the water.

Flying female

This female mallard is brown all over, whereas the male is brighter, with a green head. The female quacks more loudly than the male.

Seabirds

Some seabirds spend most of their lives soaring over the open ocean. Others search for food on the seashore. At nesting time, most cluster together on cliffs in huge groups called colonies. With birds on every level, a cliff is like a high-rise apartment building!

Puffins and pufflings

Brightly colored beaks and black-and-white feathers give puffins a special appearance. Most of their lives are spent on the open ocean. They can swim and fly. To breed, puffins travel to rocky islands where they build their nests. Their chicks are called pufflings.

A pelican's beak holds three times more fish than its stomach.

Fish scoop

Pelicans feed by diving, or by dipping their beaks under water. Their beaks have a stretchable pouch, used as a fishing net. Pelicans surface with a beakful of fish and seawater. They dribble out the water and gulp down their meal.

Seaside clowns

With their clownlike markings, laughing gulls are among the most common seaside gulls. They are named for their noisy call, which sounds like a crazy laugh.

Takeout food

Some seabirds follow fishing trawlers. They are not being sociable, just waiting to scoop up any fish that fall over the side of the boat.

The parrot family

Containing more than 300 species, the parrot family includes many of the world's most beautiful and brightly-colored birds. Some parrots live in dense tropical rain forests, others in large open plains.

A muddy meal

These noisy macaws have gathered on a mud bank in South America. It is thought that they peck at the soil and clay to get extra minerals that are missing from their everyday diet.

Flocks of pets

Sociable birds, budgerigars live in vast flocks in Australia. Although small, budgerigars can fly vast distances in hot and dry weather in search of food and water. Wild budgerigars are always green, with a yellow face and black markings.

Feathery facts

● Parrots are good climbers, using their beaks and claws to move around the branches.

● Parrots eat mainly fruit, nuts, and seeds.

● If one parrot spots food, it will alert the rest of the flock.

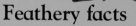

Finger food

Many birds grip their food with their feet, but parrots are the only birds that can hold food up to their beaks. Their fleshy toes act like human fingers!

The crested bird

Cockatoos are white, pink, or black. Their large head crests are raised when the birds are angry, excited, or frightened.

The fig is gripped tightly in this parrot's claws.

Loving parrots

Lovebirds live up to their name, since they are fond of sitting in pairs and preening each other! All nine species originally come from Africa and nearby islands.

Rainbow colors

Parakeets are small parrots. There are many species of these birds, living in flocks in warm and tropical areas.

Feathered but flightless

Not all birds fly, although all have evolved from flying birds. Some, like penguins, walk or hop across rocks. Others, such as ostriches, walk or run quickly across the ground.

Can't catch me!

The smaller relatives of ostriches, rheas live in South America, where they avoid predators by running. They run fast with their necks stretched almost level with the ground.

Racing roadrunners

With lightning speed, roadrunners race on foot across the desert after insects, lizards, and snakes. They can even catch and kill rattlesnakes. Roadrunners are able to fly, but prefer to run.

Hop to it

Rockhopper penguins get their name from the way they travel up rocky cliffs. They jump along with their feet together as if taking part in a sack race!

On the run

Ostriches are the tallest and heaviest birds of all. A human being only comes up to the shoulder of a large male ostrich. These giants of the bird world can run as fast as 43 mph (70 kph) in short bursts.

Penguin parade

Why aren't penguins afraid of polar bears? Because penguins make their home in the Antarctic, where there are no polar bears. Only two species, Emperor and Adélie, live in Antarctica itself, but several other varieties are found in the surrounding seas.

Safety in numbers

Antarctic penguins live in large colonies on the sea ice. Emperors, the largest variety, don't build nests, but keep their babies (called chicks) warm next to their bodies.

I'm hungry!

Penguins recognize and respond to each other's cries, which is just as well, since this Emperor baby is shouting for his supper. Both Mom and Dad store food in their stomachs, then bring it up again to feed their young.

Penguin facts

- Penguins drink both fresh- and saltwater.

- Emperors can stay under water for up to 20 minutes.

- When penguins catch fish, they swallow them whole.

- Adult Emperors are as tall as a 3- or 4-year-old child.

Water wings

Penguins eat fish and seafood. To catch it, these Emperors can dive far below the ocean's surface. They glide through the water as if they're flying, but the closest they come to real flying is when they leap out again—and belly flop on the ice!

Making a home

The smaller Adélie penguins build nests on rocky coasts and islands. The nests are made from small stones carried in the birds' beaks and dropped into place.

Smile for the camera!

Other varieties of penguin, including Gentoo, Macaroni, King, Chinstrap, and Humbolt, live nearby. This one's goofy "smile" is actually a line of black feathers under his beak. Can you guess what kind he is?   (Chinstrap)

73

The reptile house

Reptiles are scaly-skinned, "cold-blooded" creatures with a bony skeleton and a backbone. They live on land, in freshwater, and in the sea. There are four main groups of reptiles alive today.

Desert tortoises

Tortoises live on land. Turtles and terrapins live in the sea (saltwater) or in rivers and ponds (freshwater).

The *Chelonia* group

Tortoises, turtles, and terrapins are known as Chelonians. All members of this group, or "order," have a body that is protected by a shell.

Squamata everywhere!

The Squamata order contains every single species of lizard and snake. It is by far the largest group of living reptiles. Amazingly, nearly all reptiles are lizards and snakes.

Snakes may have had legs for digging down, but now

All Crocodilian reptiles, like these crocodiles, have tough, armorlike skin covering their entire bodies.

The Crocodilians

Crocodiles, alligators, caimans, and gharials all belong to the Crocodilia group. Most make their homes in warm freshwater rivers, lakes, and swamps.

The world is home to about 6,500 different reptile species.

A rare breed

Today, there is only one species of reptile remaining in the Rhynchocephalia group – the tuatara. Tuataras are only found in one area of the world – a set of small islands off the coast of New Zealand.

they wriggle around.

COLD BLOOD?

Reptiles are known as cold-blooded creatures, but they do not always have chilly blood. An animal is "cold-blooded" if its body temperature changes depending on how hot or cold the surroundings are. Reptiles bask in sunlight to heat up. This keeps the body working well. If a reptile's body is not warm enough, its stomach cannot deal with (digest) its food.

Feeling the heat

Some snakes have special gaps around their lips that are sensitive to heat. These are called heat pits. They are used to detect warm-blooded animal prey.

This emerald tree boa has lots of heat pits along its lips.

Double vision

A chameleon can move one eye, on its own, without moving the other. This means that it can look in two different directions at the same time. It can use one eye to hunt insects, and the other to look out for attackers.

Reptile file

● Snakes do not have ears on the outside. They "hear" vibrations as they travel through their jawbones and into their inner ears.

● The organ in snakes and lizards that "tastes" their environment is called the Jacobson's organ.

Sssenses

Most reptiles can see, hear, and smell, but they also have other ways of detecting things. Some reptiles rely on one sense that is very well-developed, while others use a mixture of sense skills to get by.

The taste test

A snake's tongue flicks in and out to collect up chemicals in the air. A sense organ inside the mouth "smells" and "tastes" these chemicals, helping the snake to sample food, find a mate, and to detect prey or enemies.

Snakes use their senses of smell, taste, and touch more than their eyesight and hearing.

Fully aware

Iguanas have very clear sight and full-color vision. Like most lizards, they detect sounds in the air using an eardrum in the skin behind the eye.

The eardrum is very thin and flexible.

The body heat of this rat can be sensed by a snake's heat pits.

A tale of scales

Reptile skin is covered in overlapping, waterproof plates called scales. This layer of skin is good at keeping moisture inside, so that reptiles can survive in hot, dry places.

Snake

Caiman

Skink (a lizard)

Tortoise

Sensible outfits

Skinks and snakes have smooth, flexible scales for burrowing or moving across ground. The leathery scales of caimans are strengthened by bony plates on the back and belly – while tortoises have a tough, warty covering on their head and legs.

Reptile skin does three main jobs. It keeps water out, body moisture in, and protects the creature's inside parts from injury during fights or attacks.

Spines and crests

Many reptiles have rough, granulelike scales that rise into spiked points along their back. The sharp spines are good for defense – and often form beautiful crests, which are useful for attracting a mate.

Gecko (a lizard)

Old skin, new skin

To get rid of older, worn-out scales, all reptiles shed their outer layer of skin from time to time. This is called molting or sloughing. Snakes shed their whole skin in one piece, starting at the head.

The snake's skin comes off inside out – like a sock being peeled off a human's foot.

This armored spiny lizard has conelike, spiked scales along the full length of its backbone (spine).

The skin of a reptile is not very good at holding on to body heat.

Reptile file

● A reptile's outer scales are mostly made up of something called keratin, which also goes into making human hair and fingernails.

● Lizards lose their skin bit by bit as it falls off in large flakes. Some peel it off with their mouth and eat it as food.

Scales are extra-thick pieces of skin.

Enter the dragons

In the world of reptiles, dragons really do exist. These types of lizard often have incredible features that make them just as strange as the creatures found in fairy tales.

"Hey, watch the beard..."

This bearded dragon has a set of spiked scales around its throat, just like a man's beard. The "beard" expands so that the lizard will look too big for predators to swallow.

On the run

Most lizards get around on four legs, but – like people – the crested water dragon often uses just its two back (hind) legs when making a quick escape.

All talk, no action

If in danger, the frilled lizard opens its gaping mouth and spreads out an umbrella-like frill around its neck. This is to scare away any approaching predators.

Reptile file

- The eastern water dragon of Australia escapes from its enemies by diving underwater, where it can stay for up to 30 minutes.

- The frilled lizard's bright cape is a large flap of loose skin. When opened out, it can be more than four times the width of the lizard's body.

Komodo dragons can grow to nearly 10 ft (3 m) in length.

The lizard king

Komodo dragons are the largest of all living lizards. They can catch and kill goats and pigs, but often feed on the leftovers of dead animals.

Slither slither

Along with lizards, snakes are members of the Squamata group. Snakes do not have hands and feet. Instead, they have a flexible body, which they use to wriggle and crawl over land – as well as for swimming through water. Their scales help them to grip surfaces.

Stretch marks

A snake's skeleton is simply a skull and a long, flexible backbone with ribs attached. Muscles joined to the ribs allow the snake to twist and coil its long, flexible body.

Worried rattlesnakes raise their tails...

"Buzz" off

This western diamondback rattlesnake has a poisonous bite, but it does not like to waste its venom (poison). It always uses its rattle first, hoping that this will be enough to scare off its enemy.

The vines are alive!
Green tree snakes have light, skinny bodies for creeping and climbing. Their skin color helps them to hide among green vines and foliage as they hunt for birds or tree-dwelling frogs and lizards.

and twitch the tip to rattle out a warning "buzz."

The great pretender
The milksnake (right) is harmless, but has the same set of colors as the venomous coral snake (above). Predators get confused and so prefer not to attack.

Without venom, the milksnake has to strangle (constrict) its prey.

Rubbernecks
Many snakes eat hard-shelled birds' eggs or soft-shelled reptile eggs. The African egg-eating snake only eats birds' eggs. It can unhook its jaws to swallow eggs that are at least twice the size of its head.

The hardbacks

Chelonians all have one thing in common –
the hard-shell home they carry around. Every
reptile in this group has a set of hardy
features that help it to cope with
its natural environment.

Giant tortoises
have shells up to
4 ft (1.3 m) long.

Island wonder

The giant tortoises of the
Galápagos Islands are not
bothered by the hot, dry
conditions there. They
live on bare, rocky
ground and can go
without food and
water for long
periods of time.

Reptile file

● Tortoises and turtles can
live for more than 100 years.

● The "growth rings" on a
Chelonian's bony plates help
to show how old it is.

● Some turtles can survive
for weeks underwater
without having to
come up for air.

Hard house

Chelonian shells are made of a dome-shaped top and a flatter shield under the belly. Both parts are made up of bony plates. The surface of the shell is covered in large scales called scutes.

Domed top (carapace).

Shielded belly (plastron).

Bottoms up!

Turtles push their heads above water to take in air, but can also breathe underwater. They do this by taking air in through their skin, the lining of their throat, and also through a small hole near their bottom!

European pond turtle

The giant tortoise's long neck helps it to reach up to high-growing plants.

Heads up!

Most Chelonians are able to pull their heads back into their shells for protection. If involved in a squabble, they bring their heads right out to show their anger.

These two giant tortoises are having a little argument.

Shell suits

The shells are needed for self-defense. High-arched and knobby shells give protection from bad weather and predators. Shells that blend into the natural surroundings can also help to disguise tortoises and turtles.

Starred tortoise

Alligator snapping turtle

Snake-neck turtle

Pond turtle (terrapin)

Snap

These snappy-looking creatures are large, intelligent reptiles that are well-adapted to life in the water. Crocodilians all have similar features, but there are some interesting differences, too.

The strange bump on a male's snout is called a ghara.

A gharial's teeth are all the same size and shape.

Air conditioning

A crocodile uses various tricks to control its body temperature. On a hot day, it can cool down by raising its head and opening its mouth – or by crawling away into the shade or into water.

Nile crocodile

Crocodiles are more closely related to birds than to other reptiles.

Snack attack

All Crocodilian reptiles are meat-eaters (carnivores). Even the larger crocs and gators are quick and strong enough to launch themselves out of the water – straight up into the air like a rocket – and snatch their prey.

Ganges
gharial

Scissor-face

It is easy to recognise a gharial by the shape of its head.
It has a long snout and scissorlike jaws that each contain
more than 50 teeth. This kind of head is excellent for fishing.

Gator or croc?

Alligators are not as
widespread as crocodiles.
They only live in the
southeastern US and China.
Gators have a shorter body
and snout than crocs – but
they usually live longer.

American alligator

*A crocodile's fourth
tooth sticks out when
its mouth is closed.*

Alligator junior

This is a caiman – a type of alligator from Central
and South America. The caiman is smaller than other
Crocodilians and can move much
more quickly on land. Its body
is protected by strong,
bony plates.

*Caiman teeth are sharper and
longer than alligator teeth.*

87

Land and water

Some creatures can move happily between water and land, some even living a part of their lives in water, as nymphs, before moving onto land as adults. They are called amphibians.

A Mandarin salamander eats a worm. But if someone tries to eat him his skin releases a bad taste.

I am a newt

Newts have long bodies, four limbs, soft skin, and, typically, live most of their lives on land, returning to water to breed.

I'm all grown up

The axolotl is unusual among amphibians because it doesn't develop an adult form but keeps its external gills (they are easy to spot, because they are bright red). Axolotls use their gills to breathe under water.

I am a salamander

There is little difference between salamanders and newts. Salamanders tend to live in water, while newts spend most of their time on land. But that's not always the case.

Spotted salamander

Is it a worm? No!

Caecilians are wormlike amphibians that have no arms or legs. They feed largely on earthworms. Some live in water, while others burrow into soil or leaf litter. It is rare to see one.

Like many toads, the South American ornate horned toad has warty skin.

The red tomato frog's plump shape and vivid red color give it its common name.

Sticky pads on the ends of a white tree frog's toes make it easy for the frog to climb.

Toads and frogs

Frogs and toads are probably the best-known of all amphibians, and there are many different kinds (there are more than 4,000 species). Most live in damp habitats. Brightly colored tree frogs live in rain forests.

Safety in schools
Small fish such as saupe
often swim in large groups
called schools or shoals.
There is safety in numbers!

What is a fish?

All fish have fins for swimming and gills for breathing under water. Fish also have their own suits of armor! Most are covered in overlapping scales like tiles on a roof. Some just have extra-tough skin. They are slimy so that they can glide swiftly through water.

Super senses

Fish can hear, smell, and taste. They have taste buds in their mouths, fins, and skin. This polka-dot grouper swims head down while prowling for food.

How fish breathe

On land, oxygen is in the air. Water also contains oxygen. Fish gulp water and run it over their gills. Oxygen passes through the gills into the fish's blood.

Muted color camouflages fish in the open ocean.

Fish often have excellent eyesight.

Opening to gills

Shapes and sizes of scales vary in different fish.

Swim like a fish!

Fish swim like snakes wriggle. Their bodies form S-shaped curves. Most fish use their tails for the main push forward. A few row themselves along with their fins.

Lesser spotted dogfish

Dogfish wiggle from side to side.

Fantastic fish

Fish can be weird and wonderful! They vary in size from tiny sea horses to giant manta rays. Some have unusual shapes that help them to hide or scare off predators.

Manta rays flap with wide, winglike fins and glide through the water.

Prickly beauty

Lionfish have striped bodies to warn away other fish. Any predator that bites a lionfish will be pierced by poisonous spines.

Gentle giants

The vast, flat bodies of manta rays blend in with the mud and sand of the seabed. Despite their size, manta rays are gentle creatures. They eat mainly plankton.

Hidden on the seabed

Stonefish change color to blend in with the seabed. They have spines on their backs for protection. Each spine injects a deadly poison if touched.

Puffed up

When in danger, porcupine fish gulp down water and swell up like balloons. Now they are too large and prickly for most predators to swallow!

A relaxed porcupine fish with spines lying flat.

A puffed-up porcupine fish has raised spines.

Colorful ribbon

Ribbon eels can coil themselves into crevices that seem too small for their long bodies. They have sharp teeth for seizing prey.

Eels are fish but they look much more like snakes!

Slimy, slippery skin

Dragon of the sea

Leafy sea dragons live in shallow, seaweedy waters. Here, they avoid predators by looking like seaweed. Their other name is weedy sea dragons.

Attack!

The great white shark sits at the top of the food chain. The 21 ft- (6.5 m-) long predator is dangerous to large fish and mammals, hunting seals, sea lions, and dolphins. It sometimes (though it is rare) attacks humans.

Now you see me

What color is a white shark? Silver gray! Any prey looking up from the bottom of the sea would not see the pale belly of the shark, since it blends in with sunlight reflecting on the surface of the sea.

Even the shark's teeth are scary: they are just over 1 in (3 cm) long and have a serrated edge, like a saw.

Sharks can go through thousands of teeth. When one falls out, a larger one in the row behind moves forward.

A burst of speed and the seal is caught.

It's an ambush!

A great white can't bend its body very well, so to be a successful hunter, it needs to surprise its prey. It normally cruises along at a gentle 2 mph (3 kph), but when it finds prey, the shark shoots forward at 15 mph (25 kph).

It's thought that shark attacks on people are really a case of mistaken identity. Seen from below, a surfer on a board looks a lot like a seal—the shark's intended prey.

Watch out in the water

Is the great white really as dangerous as the film *Jaws* made out? They do kill more people than any other shark species—but the attacks are rare. More people are killed by jellyfish.

Scientists can only guess at the reasons behind the hammerhead's uniquely shaped head—but it does give the shark super hunting skills.

Big brother

There are nine different hammerhead species. Great hammerheads are the biggest, at 20 ft (6 m) long. At just 5 ft (1.5 m) long, bonnethead sharks are the smallest.

The shark's nostrils are at the ends of its head, effectively giving the shark a big nose! Its sense of smell is thought to be 10 times better than in other sharks.

Big head

Scalloped hammerhead sharks have distinctive dents in the front edge of their heads. These are the most commonly seen of all hammerheads.

A lot of sense

The shark's head is covered in sensors that pick up electric signals in the water given out by all living creatures. A big head means there are lots of sensors, which helps the shark detect prey.

Time for school

During the day, scalloped hammerheads group together in large schools. Nobody knows why they do this. When night falls, they go off by themselves to hunt for food.

Hammerhead facts

● These sharks like to live in warm waters around the coast.

● In the summer, they migrate north, with young sharks swimming in groups for safety.

● The shark's wide, flat head may act as a rudder, steering the shark as it swims along.

Daring dentist

Carnivorous sharks can make friends! A barberfish eats food left in the shark's teeth, but it's not in danger: it keeps the shark clean, so it's left alone to do its job—and gets a free meal!

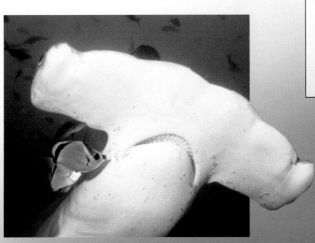

Is this the strangest shark in the sea?

Hungry hunters

Hammerheads eat all kinds of fish, including stingrays and even other sharks. They will attack turtles if given the opportunity, snapping off a flipper as a snack.

Down in the depths

No light reaches as far down as the ocean's midnight zone. Here, strange creatures live in freezing cold and total darkness. They are small so they can survive on little food.

Stretchy stomach expands if the fish lures in a big meal

Angling for fish

Angler fish have a long fishing-rod fin with a light at the end. Small fish think that this is food. Lured toward it, they swim into the angler fish's open jaws.

Fearsome hunter

The viper fish swims with its jaws open. It catches fish with its extra-long, sharp teeth.

Mouth has more than 350 lights.

Low life

Parts of the ocean floor look like the surface of the Moon Here, rattail fish dart in and out of crevices. It's easy to see how they got their name

Ugly ogre

The gruesome looks of the fangtooth explain its other name, "ogre fish." When a fish or shrimp swims past, the fangtooth sucks them into its gigantic mouth.

Large eye helps the fish to spot prey in the dark.

Shining like stars

A bladelike, silvery body gives hatchet fish their name. They have light organs along their bellies and tails.

Daggerlike teeth line the fangtooth's huge jaws.

Invertebrates

Lots of animals don't have a backbone, or any other bones. In fact, about 97 percent of all known animal species fall into this category. They are called invertebrates. Most invertebrates live in the sea, but not all.

In the air

Invertebrates have moved into every habitat you can think of, from the air around us to the soil beneath us. Most, like this butterfly, are small and have relatively short lives.

In the soil

Worms may look insignificant, but they are hugely important. They break down decaying matter, churning out the soil on which many plants depend. Earthworms are found around the world where there is soil.

Mouth parts are used for drinking fluids.

Bad invertebrates

Not all invertebrates are pretty to look at, or useful to humans. Houseflies spread a lot of disease, and fast. A female can lay up to 150 eggs a day, which quickly hatch into maggots.

A housefly's large compound eyes are made up of hundreds of small lenses.

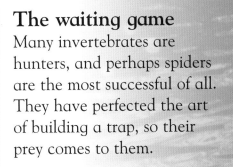

The waiting game

Many invertebrates are hunters, and perhaps spiders are the most successful of all. They have perfected the art of building a trap, so their prey comes to them.

Orb spider webs are sticky, catching any insects fast.

Amazing facts

● The largest invertebrates are giant deep-sea squid, which can reach more than 60 ft (18 m) in length.

● Invertebrate fossils have been discovered that are at least 550 million years old.

● Scientists estimate that the combined weight of all the invertebrates on our planet would outnumber humans many times.

In the sea

One of the most widely known marine invertebrates is the starfish, or sea star. These animals have a special ability: they can regenerate a lost limb. There is a huge variety of starfish, with some having more than 40 arms.

What is that?

Some marine invertebrates look more like plants than the animals they truly are. Sea anenomes fix themselves into one position and hunt from that spot using stinging tentacles.

A sea anenome has a mouth surrounded by tentacles that are covered with stinging cells.

If threatened, the sea anenome will draw in its tentacles.

Jellyfish

Adrift in the oceans since prehistoric times, jellyfish are more than 95% water. They have no brains, bones, hearts, or eyes. Their stinging tentacles act like fishing lines to catch prey.

Dinner delivered

Long tentacles trail from the jellyfish's body. When a small animal swims into them, the tentacles spear it with poisonous stings.

OCEAN DRIFTER

In warmer parts of the world, the Portuguese man-of-war drifts on the surface of the waves. It is held up by a balloonlike float. A relative of jellyfish, its other name is "blue jellyfish". It catches fish in its long tentacles. These shoot tiny stings into any animal that touches them. People are sometimes stung by a Portuguese man-of-war. The stings are not fatal to people, but they are very painful!

Underwater umbrella

Jellyfish have soft bodies called bells. The bell moves in and out like an umbrella opening and closing. This drives the jellyfish along.

Glowing jellyfish rising to the water's surface on dark nights have been mistaken for ghosts!

Jellyfish may look like a parachute but they are probably traveling upward!

Up, up, and away

Jellyfish are attracted to light even though they have no eyes. They swim toward the water's surface. This keeps them within range of food.

Fishy facts

invertebrate Despite their name, jellyfish are not fish. They are invertebrates. An invertebrate is an animal without a backbone.

transparent A transparent animal or object is one that can be seen through.

Ghostly glow

Many jellyfish are nearly transparent. Some also produce their own light, so that they glow in dark water. They may only do this when disturbed.

103

Octopuses and squid

Fast hunters, octopuses and squid have long "arms" called tentacles for seizing prey. They swim at high speed by squirting jets of water from their baglike bodies. The force drives them along. This is called jet propulsion.

Sucker-studded tentacles

Octopuses feel and taste with their eight tentacles. Each tentacle has rows of suckers. The suckers help them to grip prey and fasten themselves to the seabed.

Octopuses are intelligent with large brains.

Speedy retreat

When in danger, octopuses jet off. Their bodies form a torpedolike shape to slice through water. Like squid, they can outswim most predators.

Tentacles trail out behind the body as the octopus takes off.

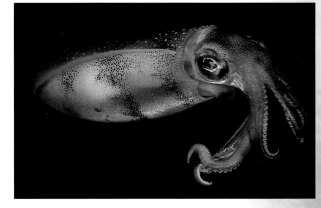

Nighttime prowler

In the daytime, octopuses hide alone in rocky dens. At night they come out to hunt. They try to keep a tentacle on the seabed. If threatened, they can pull themselves back fast.

Shimmering squid

Many squid can produce their own light. They use this light display to signal to each other or lure prey. Fire squid can even flash white, blue, yellow, and red light.

Ink attack!

To escape predators, octopuses and squid have a trick up their sleeves. They squirt out a cloud of ink. Hidden in murky water, they make a getaway.

Life on the seabed

A few seabed animals can survive along the lower seashore. Most live on the deeper seabed where they are always underwater. These creatures often look like plants but they are really animals.

Sponges can grow so big that a person could have a bath in one!

Sponges attach themselves to the seabed.

Seabed chimneys
Sponges come in strange shapes and many colors. They feed by capturing plankton as they pump water through their bodies.

Spines cover body and arms.

Starring role

Brittle stars have brittle, easily broken arms. This does not matter because they can grow new ones! Like starfish, brittle stars do not have a brain.

This common starfish has 12 arms.

Pair of tentacles helps sea slugs seek out food.

Tentacles can be pulled back inside the body.

Hungry starfish

Starfish eat mussels and clams, using the suckers on their feet to pull the shells apart. Then they push their stomachs into the gap and eat up their prey.

Row of feet

In the slow lane

Sea cucumbers crawl along the seabed at a snail's pace. They suck in food that sticks to their slimy tentacles.

Colorful character

This sea slug is called a "Spanish shawl" because it appears to have an orange fringe. The vivid colors of sea slugs warn predators that they are poisonous and taste awful.

Hard cases

Some (not all!) invertebrates have a hard outer covering called an exoskeleton. Others, if they need the protection, have a shell, which grows with them or which they find. Let's meet some of these creatures.

This horned ghost crab will have to molt soon.

Getting ready to grow!

Animals with an exoskeleton have to molt in order to grow. That means they leave the old shell and a new, hard outer layer develops. This is the way a crab grows.

The exoskeleton even covers the lobster's antennae and its eyes.

I molt, too!

Like a crab, a lobster has to molt in order to grow. It will hide while this is happening until the new exoskeleton is strong enough to protect its body.

Not so hard

Lobsters and crabs are crustaceans. So are shrimp. But shrimp don't have such a hard outer casing. This cleaner shrimp's case is so thin that it is transparent.

Compound eyes on stalks give good all-around vision.

Are you a threat?

Believe it or not, a scallop can swim. Simple eyes beneath the shell's opening sense a predator's shadow, and it will squirt a jet of water to propel itself away.

Too cramped!

A hermit crab is an unusual crab because it has a soft abdomen. It protects itself by hiding in another creature's discarded shell. It moves its home regularly, when it finds suitable (larger) mollusk shells.

Let me at that rock!

A limpet will hold tightly onto rock on the side of a rock pool. The powerful foot creates a tight suction, which is hard to break.

Have home, will travel

Slow-moving snails carry their protective homes on their backs. Vital organs, such as the heart, lung, and stomach, are inside the shell. This African giant snail is the world's largest snail.

A snail's shell will grow as the snail grows.

A snail moves by creeping forward on a muscular foot.

Bugs, bugs, bugs

Most of the bugs that you know are called arthropods, which means they have their skeleton on the outside of their bodies. There are over a million known species of arthropods on the Earth. Here are a few types to spot.

Trapped in time

We know that insects were around over 40 million years ago because some were trapped in a substance called amber, which hardened back then.

Thorax

Head

Abdomen

What is an insect?

You can spot an insect by counting its body parts and legs. They all have six legs and three body parts – a head, a thorax, and an abdomen.

What is a myriapod?

If you try counting the legs on a creepy crawly and find you can't, chances are you are looking at a myriapod, such as a millipede or centipede. They have lots of segments and lots and lots of legs!

Extreme bugs

● The petroleum fly lives in puddles of crude oil and feeds on insects that get stuck in it.

● Some midges can be put into boiling water and survive.

● Snow fleas can survive in sub-zero temperatures. If you pick one up it will die in the heat of your hand.

What is an arachnid?

All arachnids have eight legs. Watch out however, other than spiders, a lot of arachnids look like insects so count carefully.

110

What is a true bug?

These days we tend to call all creepy crawlies "bugs". But actually a true bug is a type of insect that has a long mouthpart that it pierces its food with, and uses it to suck up the inside of it.

Leapers and creepers

Some bugs are speedy, some are slow. Some bugs run and others jump. They all have their reasons why they do what they do, and a lot depends on where they live – different obstacles demand different types of movement.

High jump
The flea is the most powerful jumper of all insects. It has a little spring in its legs to enable it to jump very high. It can jump 600 times an hour for three days, when it is looking for a host.

Legging it
The green tiger beetle is the fastest insect on earth. It runs at 3½ ft (1 m) per second. It uses its speed to catch other insects and to run quickly across the hot desert sand.

Leaps and bounds
If a grasshopper or cricket is disturbed and it needs to get away, it uses its massively developed, muscle-backed legs to leap high into the air.

A grasshopper can leap 20 times the length of its body.

Looping upwards
Some caterpillars loop their way up branches. They attach their back leg suckers to the branch and stretch their bodies forward, then loop up their back, pulling the suckers upward. They can walk up some pretty steep twigs.

Keeping in step
A millipede has up to 180 pairs of legs! They all help it force its way through the soil. It has to be very coordinated when it walks, otherwise its legs bump into each other. It moves them in waves.

Buzzing around

If you hear a buzzing sound in your yard, chances are you are listening to something that stings, such as a bee or a wasp. But there's more to these buzzing bugs than meets the eye. They build some incredible homes and are excellent team players.

Collecting nectar

During the spring and summer, the honeybee flies from flower to flower to gather nectar. Back in the hive the nectar is used to make honey.

A hive of activity

Honeybees live in hives. Inside the hive they make a honeycomb, which is made out of wax from their glands. The six-sided cells that make up the honeycomb hold honey and eggs, which the queen bee lays.

Bee dance

When a worker bee finds a good nectar supply, it returns back home to the hive and does a little "figure eight" dance, which lets the other bees know where the nectar is.

114

There is a legend in China that the inventor of paper, Ts'ai Lun (AD 89-106), watched wasps while they made their paper homes and copied them. He chewed and chewed pieces of wood in the hope that he could make paper. Unfortunately it did not work well, so he swapped saliva for glue and invented the paper that we still use today.

Building a nest

Some wasps live in large nests made of paper. The queen wasp starts the nest by chewing dead wood, mixing it with saliva, and letting it dry. She then lays some eggs, which hatch, and the next generation continuing with the nest-building.

Sweet tooth

Wasps love sugar and especially sweet fruits, which is why they buzz around your food in the summer, annoying you. They won't sting you, however, unless you threaten them.

Army of helpers

Ants and termites each live in huge colonies where they build their homes together, work together, and never have time for play. Their whole life revolves around bringing up their young safely.

Loyal subjects
The queen termite is a huge, ugly, egg-laying machine that never moves from her royal chamber. The termites rally around her, feeding and cleaning her.

Termite high-rise
Some species of termite live in huge mounds that they build using soil, saliva, and their droppings. The mounds can be up to 20 ft (6 m) high.

The king termite lives with the queen in her nest.

Firm friends

Ants and aphids are very good at keeping each other happy. The aphids eat a lot of tree sap and give off a sweet liquid that the ants like to sip. In return the ants guard them fiercely from predators.

Big bully

The toughest ant around is the Australian bulldog ant. It grips its meal in its huge, powerful jaws then swings its body around and stings the prey from behind. Bugs that get in his way don't stand a chance!

THE ANT CLEANING SERVICE

Every so often villagers in Africa receive visits from a march of up to 22 million driver ants, which forces them out of their homes. Although each ant is only 1/3 in (1 cm) long and blind, they kill every pest that gets in their way, such as locusts and scorpions. The villagers welcome the clean up!

Lots of bugs like to eat aphids, so having ant bodyguards is the best way for them to survive.

Teamwork

Some ants build their nests by weaving together groups of leaves. They each carry a live ant larva in their jaws and make it produce silk, which they then use to sew up the leaves. If anyone threatens the nest, they attack by biting.

117

Water world

If you find a body of water, chances are it's filled with minilife – but you may have to look closely to see some of it. Many bugs live in or above the water, and some can even walk on the surface.

Diving in

The diving beetle is the great meat eater of the water. It tucks a bubble of air under its wings so it can breathe underwater, and dives down to catch tadpoles and even small fish.

Walking on water
Pond skaters can walk on water because of thick, waterproof hairs on their feet. They skim over the surface looking for floating food.

Darting around
The beautiful dragonfly lives above water. It is called the dragonfly because of its very aggressive "dragon-like" behavior.

Bottoms up!
Mosquito larvae live in the water. When they need air, they swim to the surface and hang there with their snorkel-like breathing tubes poking up through the top.

Back stroke
The water boatman hangs upside down just beneath the surface. It looks like a little boat, and its back legs are just like oars, which is how it got its name.

Caddis armor
The larva of the caddis fly builds a case around itself to protect it. It makes the case out of stones, shells, and pieces of plants.

Watery web
The air-breathing water spider makes a diving bell to live in. It weaves a web under water, among the plants, and stocks it with air from the surface.

As dusk falls...

As day turns into night, some insects are just starting to wake up. Whether they are trying to keep from being eaten, or getting ready for a meal, night is a pretty lively time in bug land.

Moon moth
The first time it flies, the Indian moon moth takes to the air after dark to avoid being eaten. It doesn't have a mouth because it only lives long enough to survive on the food it ate when it was a caterpillar.

The spider also holds its net in the air, ready to catch insects.

Light fantastic

Fireflies and glowworms use a special organ in their tummies to flash light signals in order to communicate with each other. Sometimes hundreds gather together to attract mates, and can be seen for miles, like the ones in this tree.

Web master

The netcasting spider weaves its fatal net before dark. Then at nightfall it hangs upside down and drops it on any delicious insect that wanders past.

Dark stories

● The cicada's clicking sound can often be heard at dusk. It has a flap under its stomach that clicks loudly at very high speeds.

● Moths are attracted to artificial light because they use the Moon to navigate and confuse lights with the Moon.

Glowworm

Glowworms are not worms, they are beetles. This female glowworm cannot fly. It glows all the time to attract insects to its light so that it can catch and eat them.

Weird and wonderful

There are so many bugs that have evolved mysterious habits and strange looks that they could fill a whole book. Here is a small selection from around the world.

How weird would it be to have eyes on the end of stalks?

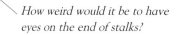

Eyes on stalks

The eyes of stalk-eyed flies are on the top of long stalks. When two males meet they compare eyes and the one with the widest set gets the girl.

Terrifying taste

The flambeau butterfly has very strange taste in food. It sits on an alligator's eyes and sips its tears. What a very brave little bug.

Stick your neck out

Why does the giraffe weevil have such a long neck? No one knows. But it certainly makes it one of the weirdest looking bugs.

Mystical mantis

You can barely tell which way around this mantis nymph is facing. If you look carefully, however, you can just see its head on the right-hand side. Its strange coloring helps it to camouflage itself.

Out of this world
If you came across this katydid (a type of bush cricket) in the jungle, you'd be forgiven for thinking that we'd just been invaded by aliens, with its spiny body and strange colors.

All change

Some insects start their lives looking completely different from their adult shape. When they are ready, certain insects, such as caterpillars, have a sudden change and emerge with a new image. Others change slowly and steadily.

1 Caterpillar stage

The blue morpho butterfly starts off as a small, hairy caterpillar, which eats and eats and eats until...

2 Pupa stage

...it sheds its skin and creates a pupa. A transformation happens inside, and one day...

4 Butterfly

...it stretches out its crumpled wings and flies away as a beautiful butterfly. The change is called metamorphosis and happens to many creatures in the insect world.

3 Emerging

...the pupa splits and a completely new-looking insect starts to emerge. It pushes itself out until...

Skin shedding
Some insects change slowly as they grow up, such as this dragonfly. Because insects have their skeletons, which don't grow, on the outside of their bodies, it means that they have to replace their skins in order to grow bigger. This dragonfly is shedding its skin for the last time.

Glossary

Adaptation a feature that allows an animal to survive in its habitat.

Algae plants that live in water. They have no roots, stems, or leaves. Seaweed is a sea algae.

Amphibian an animal that can live in and out of water.

Arthopod an animal with jointed legs and a body divided into segments, covered by a hard outer skeleton.

Breeding when animals give birth to young.

Camouflage the way animals hide by blending in with their natural surroundings.

Carnivore an animal that eats the flesh of another animal.

Cold-blooded an animal that uses its natural surroundings to warm up or cool down.

Crustacean a type of invertebrate with jointed limbs, such as a crab, lobster, or shrimp.

Display showing off parts of the body to attract a mate or defend a territory.

Echinoderms animals with spiny skins and tiny tube feet.

Sea cucumbers, sea urchins, and starfish are echinoderms.

Evolution over very long periods of time, all creatures develop different skills and features that help them cope with, or adapt to, their habitat. This is known as evolution.

Habitat the natural home and surroundings of a living creature.

Herbivore a plant eater.

Hibernate the time some animals spend asleep in the winter.

Insect an animal with three parts to its body and six legs.

Invertebrate an animal without a backbone.

Mammal a warm-blooded animal that breathes in oxygen from the air. Female mammals produce milk to feed their young.

Marsupial mammals whose young are born undeveloped. Most continue their development in a pouch.

Migration a long journey that some animals undergo each year to find better living conditions.

Nocturnal active at night.

Mollusks animals that have a soft body and no backbone.

Omnivore an animal that eats plants and meat.

Predator an animal that hunts other animals for food.

Prey an animal that is hunted by other animals for food.

Reptile an animal that has scales and lays eggs.

Rodent mammals that have strong front teeth for gnawing.

Skeleton the bony framework that supports and protects an animal's body.

Species a group of animals or plants made of related individuals who are able to produce fertile young.

Territory an area defended by an animal, or animals, against others of its kind.

Tundra flat, treeless areas that appear in regions near the Arctic and Antarctic, where thin soil lies on frozen ground.

Vertebrate an animal with a backbone.

Warm-blooded an animal that can keep its body temperature at a constant level.

Index

Acknowledgments

Dorling Kindersley would like to thank:
Dorian Spencer Davies, Beehive Illustrations (Andy Cooke), and Emily Bolam for their original artwork illustrations.

Picture credits:

The publisher would like to thank the following for their kind permission to reproduce their photographs:

(Key: a-above; b-below/bottom; c-center; f-far; l-left; r-right; t-top)

Alamy Images: Arco Images GmbH 39cl, 40ca, 109cl; Blickwinkel 101cr, 101tl; Bruce Coleman Inc. / Bruce Coleman Ltd 65; Bryan & Cherry Alexander Photography 47tr; Buschkind 88cl; Bruce Coleman Inc 88cr; Bill Coster 2-3; David Fleetham 94tr, 95clb; Robert Harding Picture Library Ltd / Thorsten Milse 38cra; Jeff Rotman 96ftl; Steve Bloom Images 20-21, 39t, 43tl; tbkmedia.de 41r; WoodyStock 100bl. **Ardea:** John Cancalosi 10cra; Jean-Paul Ferrero 42; Stefan Meyers 36-37b; Sid Roberts 27t; Steffen & Alexandra Sailer 38l; Adrian Warren 27cr. **Ryan Backman:** 109cr. **Trevor Barrett:** 34tl. **Ashley J. Boyd:** 17br. **brandoncole.com:** 53tr. **Bryan and Cherry Alexander Photography:** 8bl, 72-73, 73cb; Mark Ryan 72l; Frank Todd 9br. **Mark Cawardine:** 15br. **Chris Gomersall Photography:** 66-67b. **Bruce Coleman Inc:** Mark Newman 47tl. **Phillip Colla / OceanLight.com:** 48bl. **Mark Conlin:** 50b. **Corbis:** Niall Benvie 41bl; Jonathan Blair 86bl; Markus Botzek / Zefa 59tr; Tom Brakefield / Zefa 1; Ralph A. Clevenger 48-49; Nigel J. Dennis / Gallo Images 21tr; Nigel J. Dennis / Gallo Images 41t; Stephen Frink 87cr; Martin Harvey / Gallo Images 18cr; Eric and David Hosking 69cl; Steve Kaufman 66bl; Layne Kennedy 22cr; Joe McDonald 49tr, 76t; Robert Pickett 28; Galen Rowell 9tl; Paul A. Souders 22tl; Hans Strand 7tr; Jeff Vanuga 28br. **David Tipling Photo Library:** Arthur Morris 64br; David Tipling 66cr. **DK Images:** Hunstanton Sea Life Centre 48c; Jeremy Hunt - modelmaker 7cb (shark); Natural History Museum, London 94cr; Jerry Young 7ca (wolf), 7tl (polar bear), 38c. **FLPA:** Tui De Roy / Minden Pictures 84-85; Michael & Patricia Fogden / Minden Pictures 10b; Tom and Pam Gardner 11tl; Mitsuaki Iwago / Minden Pictures 24cb; Gerard lacz 24-25, 31tr; Chris Mattison 78-79, 83ca; Elliott Neep 7br; Chris Newbert / Minden Pictures 7ftl (turtle); Pete Oxford 39br; Silvia Reiche 89c; Malcolm Schuyl 126-127; Konrad Wothe 40b; Norbert Wu / Minden Pictures 73tr, 99cb. **Jeff Foott:** 107br. **Getty Images:** Tom Brakefield 23; Michael & Patricia Fogden 89t; Gallo Images / Wolfgang Kaehler 44cr; The Image Bank - Anup Shah 37tl; The Image Bank / Kevin Schafer 46b; Minden Pictures / ZSSD 44tl; National Geographic / Annie Griffiths Belt 45; National Geographic / Walter Meayers Edwards 36tl; Panoramic Images 4-5b; Riser / Joseph Van Os 22bl; Stone / Art Wolfe 59tl; Telegraph Colour Library 92. **Charles and Sandra Hood:** 102cr.

Imagestate: 34-35; Mark Newman 73br; Pictor 26l, 53b. **A. Kerstitch:** 107tl. **Joe McDonald:** 14cla. **Rosanna Milligan:** 109tr. **Natural Visions:** Heather Angel 31bl. **naturepl. com:** Peter Bassett 49b; Jeff Foot 70cra; Tony Heald 71; Dietmar Nill 60cl; Premaphotos 117bl. **NHPA / Photoshot** Anthony Bannister 38bl, 121bc; George Bernard 74-75; Mark Bowler 43tr; James Carmichael Jr. 13cl; Stephen Dalton 112tr, 112-113 (grasshoppers); Martin Harvey 24bl, 76cl, 108t; Daniel Heuclin 11bl; Image Quest 3-D 103clb; Hellio & Van Ingen 85cra; T. Kitchin & V. Hurst 30; L Hugh Newman 68cr; Haroldo Palo Jnr 122tr; Peter & Beverly Pickford 116; Rod Planck 70br; Dr. Ivan Polunin 120-121; Kevin Schafer 35tr; Jonathan & Angela Scott 20tl; Mirko Stelzner 68; Robert Wu 98tr. **Pacific Stock:** 52, 104t, 105cra, 106t. **Photolibrary:** AlaskaStock 37ftr; Jack Clark 111; Paulo de Oliveira 113tl; L & D Jacobs 18-19; Satoshi Kuribayashi 114tl; London Scientific Films 125; OSF 98clb, 106b; OSF / Clive Bromhall 43cl; OSF / David B. Fleetham 103tr; OSF / David Fleetham 50cla; OSF / G Bernard 119bl; OSF / Howard Hall 102-103b, 103tc; OSF / John Mitchell 86c; OSF / Kathie Atkinson 117tl; OSF / Mantis Wildlife Films / Densey Clyne 121tr; OSF / Maurice Tibbles 32bl, 59b; OSF / Michael Fogden 11c; OSF / Mike Hill 18tl; OSF / Peter Lillie 43; OSF / Robert A. Tyrrell 55clb; OSF / Stan Osolinski 62l; OSF/ Tammy Peluso 105crb; OSF / Tobias Bernhard 50cr; OSF/ Tom Ulrich 75ca; OSF / Tui de Roy 85c; OSF / Zig Leszczynski 83tl; Herb Segars 102tl. **Photoshot / Woodfall Wild Images:** Bob Gibbons 86-87. **Premaphotos Wildlife:** Ken Preston-Mafham 122fcla. **Andrew Purcell:** 90-91, 118b. **Dr. Friede Sauer:** 102bc. **Science Photo Library:** Tony Camacho 29c, 44br; Darwin Dale 121tl; Manfred Danegger / Okapia 63b; E. R. DEGGINGER 63tl; Gregory Dimijian 27bl; Bernhard Edmaier 9cra; Eye of Science 100br; Douglas Faulkner 51; Adam Jones 19tr; Stephen J. Krasemann 56-57; Stephen J. Krasemann / Nature Conservatory 26r; Leonard Rue Enterprises 40c; George Ranalli 67t; Dr. Morley Read 123; Gregory K. Scott 57tr. **SeaPics.com:** 96cl, 96cra, 97bl, 97c, 97tl; Doc White 46tl. **Shutterstock:** Jan Coetzee 29b; Eric Isselée 29tr; Seleznev Oleg 6bl. **Southampton Oceanography Centre:** 98-99b. **Still Pictures:** Andre Bartschi 13cr; Biosphoto / Klein J.-L. & Hubert M.-L. 25tl; Brunner-UNEP 35bl; Roland Seitre 32-33; Michael Sewell 47br. **SuperStock:** Age Fotostock 36cr. **Kim Taylor:** 61c.

Jacket images: *Front:* **Corbis:** DLILLC fclb; Jenny E. Ross t. **Getty Images:** Paul Oomen fcrb. **NHPA / Photoshot:** Kevin Schafer crb. **SeaPics.com:** cb. **SuperStock:** Ingram Publishing clb. *Back:* **Corbis:** Jenny E. Ross t (knock back). **Shutterstock:** Justin Black cb, fclb; Jose Gil clb; Krishnacreationz fcrb; Kristian Sekulic crb. *Spine:* **Shutterstock:** Cofkocof.

All other images © Dorling Kindersley
For further information see: www.dkimages.com